Mental Toughness Mindset

Develop an Unbeatable Mind, Self-Discipline, Iron Will, Confidence, Will Power - Achieve the Success of Sports Athletes, Trainers, Navy SEALs, Leaders and Become Unstoppable

Stephen Patterson

© **Copyright 2019 - All rights reserved.**

The content contained within this book may not be reproduced, duplicated or transmitted without direct written permission from the author or the publisher.

Under no circumstances will any blame or legal responsibility be held against the publisher, or author, for any damages, reparation, or monetary loss due to the information contained within this book. Either directly or indirectly.

Legal Notice:
This book is copyright protected. This book is only for personal use. You cannot amend, distribute, sell, use, quote or paraphrase any part, or the content within this book, without the consent of the author or publisher.

Disclaimer Notice:

Please note the information contained within this document is for educational and entertainment purposes only. All effort has been executed to present accurate, up to date, and reliable, complete information. No warranties of any kind are declared or implied. Readers acknowledge that the author is not engaging in the rendering of legal, financial, medical or professional advice. The content within this book has been derived from various sources. Please consult a licensed professional before attempting any techniques outlined in this book.

By reading this document, the reader agrees that under no circumstances is the author responsible for any losses, direct or indirect, which are incurred as a result of the use of information contained within this document, including, but not limited to, — errors, omissions, or inaccuracies.

Contents

Introduction _____ 1

Chapter 1:
Discover the Champion Mindset_____ 3

Chapter 2:
Improve Your Self-Confidence_____ 13

Chapter 3:
Improve Your Self-Discipline _____ 25

Chapter 4:
Improve Your Attitude_____ 37

Chapter 5:
Improve Your Control of Negative Emotions _____ 47

Chapter 6:
Improve Your Leadership Skills _____ 59

Chapter 7:
Improve Your Emotional Intelligence _____ 69

Chapter 8:
Improve Your Ability to Remain in Control _____ 81

Chapter 9:
Improve Your Ability to Trust Your Instincts _____ 91

Chapter 10:
Improve Your Mental Fortitude _____ 101

Chapter 11:
Improve Your Assertiveness _____ 113

Chapter 12:
Improve Your Ability to Set Goals Successfully_____ 123

Conclusion _____ 133

MENTAL
— TOUGHNESS —
MINDSET

DEVELOP AN UNBEATABLE MIND, SELF-DISCIPLINE, IRON WILL, CONFIDENCE, WILL POWER - ACHIEVE THE SUCCESS OF SPORTS ATHLETES, TRAINERS, NAVY SEALS, LEADERS AND BECOME UNSTOPPABLE

STEPHEN PATTERSON

Introduction

Have you ever wondered what sets the best of the best apart from the rest? The truth is it isn't that they are stronger, smarter or more capable, it's that they have a unique mindset that encourages them not to give up, regardless of the adversity.

While this mindset is innate in some people, the rest of us are still in luck as it is also something that can be learned. As such, the following chapters will provide you with everything you need to know in order to instill yourself with the essence of the champion's mind. You will learn to hone aspects of yourself including your self-confidence, self-discipline, attitude, emotional control, leadership, emotional intelligence, your ability to remain in control regardless of the situation, your ability to tune in to your intuition, your overall mental fortitude, your assertiveness and your ability to set and follow through on goals.

Stephen Patterson

Chapter 1:
Discover the Champion Mindset

As children, some people are told they excel in certain subjects while others are told that they succeeded because they tried hard and that effort leads to success. The first group of children can be expected to develop a fixed mindset whereby their brains become more active when they are being told how well they have done. The second group of children can be said to have a growth mindset wherein their minds are the most active when they are learning what they could do better next time. Those with a fixed mindset tend to worry more about how they are seen by others than what they are learning which is why those with a growth mindset tend to be more successful in the long run.

Fixed Mindset
- Wants to look smart or competent regardless of the reality
- Quick to avoid challenges
- Easily thwarted by obstacles
- Thinks effort is "pointless"
- Ignores feedback
- Can feel threatened by the success of others

Growth Mindset
- More interested in long-term results.
- Enjoys a challenge.
- Learns from obstacles
- Equates effort with success
- Appreciates criticism
- Finds inspiration in the success of others

Mental Toughness Mindset

The two mindsets also manifest themselves differently when it comes to dealing with setbacks. When those who have a fixed mindset are met with a setback it directly affects how they see themselves because it shakes their belief in their innate talent. This makes it easier for them to give up on something they are struggling with as they can easily tell themselves that it is just not a talent that is in their wheelhouse. On the other hand, when a person with a growth mindset is met with a challenge, they instead worry about the best way to overcome it and treat the issue as an opportunity to learn and grow.

Those with a fixed mindset believe themselves to have a set level of ability which means that if they cannot surpass an obstacle on the first try, there is no reason for them to try again because nothing about the scenario will ever change. It doesn't take much to see how this type of reductive mindset can make it difficult to start working your way out of a difficult situation as it can make it seem like there is no point in even getting started. On the other hand, those with a growth mindset always appreciate a good challenge for the opportunity to overcome it and learn from the experience.

Change your mind: In order to change your personal outlook, you will need to learn to take advantage of the brain's neuroplasticity. Years ago, it was thought that the brain only developed during childhood. However, modern studies have discovered and proven that the brain does not lose its ability to program itself, even in adulthood. It simply takes more effort when it happens later in life, but it is, nonetheless, still possible. Studies show that not only can the brain be programmed in its thinking, but even the physical structure of the brain will change in the process of learning new information and behaviors.

In order to go from a fixed to a growth mindset, the first thing that you are going to want to do is to take an analytical look at your life and see which habits you currently take for granted are enabling this destructive mindset to perpetuate itself. Once you have really looked at how you act daily it will be much easier to determine how you can counteract them for the better. The easiest way to get started is through a dedicated diet of repetition.

Changing your mindset is all about committing to the task at hand and changing small thoughts regarding your ability to change in general. Over time, you will be able to consciously alter larger thoughts which will then make it easier to take more active control over your mindset.

When working to keep a growth mindset in all things, it is important to keep it up even when the going gets tough. It will likely seem like the easiest thing in the world to do while things are going well, but a fixed mindset is much more likely to manifest itself during times when roadblocks begin presenting themselves. Your fixed mindset will likely make you want to abandon all hope of forward progress when these roadblocks appear.

In this case, it is important to try to stop thinking of the challenges as roadblocks and start thinking of them as opportunities for you to learn and grow. Finding personal ways to meet the challenges that come your way head on without dwelling on them unnecessarily is the first step towards making a real change for the better.

Once you have begun to change your faulty habits it is important to have a broad understanding of how long the change will take. The easier the bad habit is to engage in the more difficult it will be to change which is why having a general idea of the timetable for such can make working through it much easier. During this time, it will also be important to make a mental list of places or activities which trigger the bad habit and avoid them when at all possible. Finding yourself in a situation where you are face to face with the things which trigger your bad habit is a surefire way to slip up and fall back into old habits.

Making the extra effort to ensure that you remain motivated no matter how long the process takes is no easy feat, but you should find that keeping your eye on the end goal will make the entire process seem that much easier. Then, after a timeline has been established in regard to how long it will likely take for you to form your new habits you will want to add in smaller milestones that you can look forward to in order to prove to yourself that you are making progress, regardless of what the moment to moment might feel like. Keep in mind that even the most complicated habits rarely take more than 10 weeks to form which means that if you are having trouble getting something to stick then you may have simply not been trying for long enough.

Be grateful: While making a concentrated effort to be more grateful might seem like an odd way to improve your mindset, studies show that this feeling is linked to additional feelings related to an overall improved quality of life, less stress and even less pronounced signs of aging. In fact, those with a more grateful attitude are also known to have a lower average blood pressure and lower overall levels of aggression as well. As such, if you make it a point to start each day off gratefully then developing a more grateful attitude, in general, will happen as a result. In order to jumpstart the process, consider the following tips.

Writing a handwritten letter to a friend or loved one to thank them for a recent act of kindness will not only make their day, but it will also help you to get in the habit of being grateful for the little things in life. It is important that this letter is handwritten as it makes the entire act less spontaneous and more focused. Taking the extra time will also make it easy for you to reflect on what it is you are truly grateful for.

Along similar lines, you may also find it useful to purchase a physical calendar and write five things you are thankful for on it every day for a year. Not only will doing so help you always go a long way towards being grateful, but it will also make it easy to find inspiration during times when you otherwise feel as though you don't have anything to be grateful for.

You should also get into the habit of thinking about every experience you have each day as its own type of gift. Make a concentrated effort for a week to thank the universe each day for the things you regularly enjoy but frequently accept without thinking twice about them. Thank the universe for a beautiful sunrise, your morning tea or even the challenges you face throughout the day. After you spend a week or more focusing on being grateful for the little things you will find that you are more grateful in general without even thinking twice about it.

You may also want to consider what major events you have coming up in the relatively near future so that you can spend some time each day focusing on how grateful you are that this thing is going to come to pass and that you get to enjoy it. When the first event does come to fruition, don't rest on your laurels and instead pick another activity or event that you can be grateful for soon and start the process all over again.

Stephen Patterson

Chapter 2:
Improve Your Self-Confidence

Building self-confidence is a dream that many people have, yet it is something that few pursue. This is because, like anything worth doing, getting started building self-confidence can be quite difficult especially if you have very little of it to begin with. Regardless of your current level of self-confidence, however, there are several simple yet productive thought exercises you can practice forcing your mind into the habit of thinking about things in the proper self-confident light.

Building self-confidence is a dream that many people have, yet it is something that few pursue. This is because, like anything worth doing, getting started building self-confidence can be quite difficult especially if you have very little of it to begin with. Regardless of your current level of self-confidence, however, there are several simple yet productive thought exercises you can practice forcing your mind into the habit of thinking about things in the proper self-confident light.

Think About Where Your Fears Actually Come From

When it comes time to assert yourself, if you find yourself becoming afraid, instead, you must first force yourself to understand that the only way this fear will ever leave you is if you master it completely. If you're still having trouble, consider the following tips for success:

Reframe your anxiety: If you are uncertain about the outcome of an event, that uncertainty can manifest itself as anticipation which is just a hair's breadth from fear. Reacting in a scenario that would benefit from self-confidence with anxiety instead, will destroy any momentum that you may have previously developed.

As such, you may find it helpful to react to your anxiety as if it were curiosity. Instead of being anxious about an outcome you can instead trick your mind into being curious as to the results instead. Curiosity and self-confidence go together much more easily than anxiety and self-confidence and you may find that curiously helps your confident momentum continue.

Take the time to decide why you are afraid: If you find yourself always responding to situations that require self-confidence in the same fearful pattern. Consider this, the human mind loves to find patterns, even when no true pattern exists. This means you may be responding to an established pattern and not actually the specifics of the current situation.

Think about the what could really happen: Another reason that many people find themselves unable to exercise self-confidence in social situations is that they let their minds get out of control when it comes to considering all the possible things that could go wrong in a given situation. While considering all the options isn't inherently a bad thing, the fact of the matter is that most of these worse-case scenarios are extremely unlikely to ever come true. Instead of letting your mind get carried away, a better course of action is to look at the situation a second time as a means of determining if things are as terrible as they first appeared. Nine times out of ten you are going to discover that the truth is far more manageable than the initial round of possibilities that you came up with.

While you might find it difficult to conceive of a world where whatever minor social faux pas you have committed is not the object of ridicule by those around you, the simple truth is that most people are too wrapped up in their own problems to worry about whatever it is that you are doing. While the moment where you try and fail may be burned into your brain, odds are no one else will even remember it tomorrow. Remember, you don't need to be on guard against failure, it is a part of life; what you do need to be on guard against is apathy that makes you reject the notion of getting back up and trying again.

Don't Just Think About It

While thinking about how you are going to be more confident in the future is easy, it won't do much for you when it comes to taking actions that are perceived as confident by those around you. Unfortunately, taking those steps is much more difficult than simply thinking about them and the only thing that mitigates this is the fact that stepping out of your comfort zone for the first time is tricky, and potentially terrifying for everyone who first sets out to try it.

The good news is that if you persevere it will get easier every time you do it.

To help you to get over the initial hump, consider the following:

Refocus: Whenever you find yourself hesitating prior to being confident in any situation, the first thing you should do before shying away is to give yourself an extra moment to think it through. Think about how being confident in the given situation would dramatically improve the circumstances you currently find yourself in and how much better your life would then be because of it. Furthermore, consider how much better your life would be if you approached every single situation in this confident manner. While this little boost of persuasion might not seem like much on paper, in practice you will be surprised at just how effective it can be. Give it a try for a few weeks and you will be well on your way to building a confident habit.

Don't worry about the consequences: The thing that trips up many people when they are trying to be confident is thinking too much about the potential negative consequences that could come about from a confident action. They end up stuck in their own heads, unable to make any move and the time for confidence passes them by. One of the quickest ways to mitigate this problem is to simply act confidently first before your brain can muster up a reason to talk you down. When you find yourself approaching a scenario where you would benefit from being confident, act first and think later, you can worry about what happens next later.

Love Yourself
When it comes to being confident in who you are, a big part of that is learning to truly accept yourself for who you are and all the various weaknesses or strengths that go into that. While it may seem basic, the truth of the matter is that a good round of self-analysis will make finding the self-confidence and even the personal empowerment you are looking for much easier to find.

A good way to go about taking an accurate count of what you are working with is to start by standing in front of a large mirror and then disrobing so that you are standing in front of yourself completely naked. While this might sound extreme, it is important to go through with it and really look at what it is you are looking at. Most people have a dramatically different view of themselves in their minds compared to the reality and this is a chance to ensure your expectations are completely aligned with reality. It is important to consider both the areas that you traditionally consider your strengths, as well as your weaknesses and to really drink it all in. You don't need to necessarily enjoy everything you see; you just need to have a clear and honest picture of the truth in your mind.

If you come across numerous flaws in this area that you feel are completely unacceptable, the best course of action is likely going to be taking it upon yourself to ensure those flaws will not bother you in the future. Regardless if this means cutting out a few favorite foods you overindulge in from time to time or if it means starting a complete diet and exercise overhaul, you will be surprised at making a positive change when it comes to taking care of yourself can make it easier to be more confident and self-empowered almost right from the start.

Consider how you feel about perfection: No one, not even the most confident person you know, can be perfect all the time. This is a fact that everyone knows but few people believe. It is easy to only view others, especially those who embody traits we envy, as never failing at anything they try while at the same time ballooning our own imperfections to extreme proportions. In these situations, it is important to remember that the mind is more likely to remember our own mistakes than those of others which means the things we don't even remember happening to others may well be enough to cause them to have their own issues with confidence. If this is the case, then it also means that they do not remember our own mistakes with any clarity so we should not focus on them as much either.

Don't compare yourself to others: Comparing yourself to those who seem to embody all the traits that you covet is an unhealthy exercise that will only produce biased results. Unless you are intimately familiar with the person you are comparing yourself to, the odds are good that you are only seeing one side of the story. You might be seeing that other person only at their best with no possible way of understanding their own struggles and personal roadblocks. What's more, any problems you are aware of will seem more minor than your own due to perception bias. The next time you go to compare yourself to someone else, stop. Take that time to come up with a few reasons to appreciate yourself instead.

Confidence in Action

After you begin to feel more confident, the next step is to learn to express it appropriately. With practice, you will find that speaking up for yourself in verbal and physical situations will allow you to find out more about how to project your confidence. How you interact with those around you is a clear representation of how confident you feel. Your goal should be to be protective of your rights and the rights of those around you while at the same time not being overly aggressive and forcing others to do things, they are not comfortable with.

It is important to know when to speak up in social situations, especially if your level of self-confidence has yet to improve very far. Failing to speak up when you are otherwise entitled to reinforce negative thought patterns including projecting negative thoughts and looking for approval in others and modifying your own needs to suit other people. It is important to always stand up for yourself as this shows others that you are a valuable and worthwhile person who deserves to be treated as such.

When asserting yourself it is important to do so appropriately and to give yourself a moment to prepare before jumping right in. It is important to take the time to ensure that you are in the right when it comes to a perceived slight and after that to gather your energy and your thoughts for the coming confrontation. If you are approaching another person, it is important to use authoritative body language. Hold your head up high, keep your back straight, let your arms hang naturally and set your feet firmly a moderate distance apart.

As you approach the other person, it is important to always speak in a clear and assertive tone that is commanding but not haughty. You want to project the fact that you are in control of the situation because you are self-confident, not conceited.

This means you will want to walk with a straight back and your head held high. When you stand in front of the other person you are going to want to square your feet and your shoulders and let your arms naturally hang at your sides. When you speak, make sure to make eye contact with the other person and avoid crossing your arms at all costs as this is often considered a sign of weakness.

Speak your mind: When you do talk to the other party you are going to want to ensure that you use a voice that is calm but still authoritative and a little bit quitter than your normal speaking voice. Making the other person strain to hear you is a power play as it means they automatically must let you control the situation in order to know what is going on. The tone that you use is extremely important as it needs to make the other person believe that obeying you is the logical choice of action. Making it clear to other people that you are confident is all about letting them know that you are in control of the current situation. When you start speaking you want to make it clear what your issue is and then follow up directly with how you plan to rectify it, so the conversation starts with all the elements clearly laid on the table.

During this discussion, it is important to keep in mind that your end goal should not be to ensure that you win out at the expense of anyone else involved, being self-confident doesn't mean always getting your way; it is more about directing the conversation in a way that solves the initial issue in the most effective way possible.

Stephen Patterson

Chapter 3:
Improve Your Self-Discipline

When it comes to achieving the goals and happiness that you want out of life, there is one simple thing you can do that will increase your chances of success 10-fold: improve your self-discipline. While the requirements to achieve your goals will vary based on the specifics, they will all have one thing in common, dedication and hard work will get you there, and self-discipline will make it possible.

Studies show that the more self-discipline and self-control a person has, the happier that person is as they tend to feel as though they are generally more prepared for anything that life can throw at them. This is because, while those without self-discipline spend time motivating themselves to do things, those with self-discipline simply did them which makes them more productive overall.

While those who lack self-discipline likely think that it is an innate behavior, in all actuality it is a skill which means that like any skill it can be improved with practice over time. There are a number of ways that you can strengthen your resolve and improve your ability to maintain your self-discipline even when it may seem difficult or impossible to do so; first, however, you must understand that it is up to you, and no one else, to make better choices in the first place. Your future self is directly influenced by what you choose to do in the present, do yourself a favor and choose wisely.

When it comes to exercising your self-discipline, especially in a scenario that will require significant time and energy to completely successfully, it is completely natural for your mind to come up with excuses as to why it makes sense to take the easy way out, some of them might even be rather believable. If you find that you are regularly putting off various tasks because of a fear of overexerting yourself, due to external factors or because you simply have too much on your plate then you may need to reevaluate your schedule and see what is really important to you before moving forward.

Internal motivation: If you hope to someday to use your self-discipline to do great things then it is important you work to foster the type of mental fortitude that will make it possible for you to treat it like a job at all times. Being your own boss means that there will never be anyone looking over your shoulder or forcing you to get to work when there are things that you would rather be doing instead. Rather, that motivation to succeed will need to come from within and will need to motivate you to do what you need to do day in and day out. Only by fueling your personal drive for success will you be able to improve and stick with it even when the going gets tough. Self-discipline isn't something that can be used halfway, you either can keep yourself in check or you don't, there is no room for middle ground.

Commit completely: When you start out down the path to self-discipline it is important to dedicate yourself to the admittedly monumental task ahead of you. Commit to the idea fully and without reservation as once you do the day to day interactions you must undertake to pursue your chosen course of action become much easier. Try making a promise on something you hold dear or even just yourself, whatever it may be; by dedicating yourself to the task at hand will make it that much easier to drown out any voices of dissension or excuses your mind might put forth to allow you an easy out from your goal. If you do not commit completely you run the risk of giving up and returning to negative habits and losing months or even years of work.

Understand your weaknesses: Everyone has common triggers that lead to negative behaviors especially those opposed to a highly self-disciplined lifestyle. When first starting out with the goal of improving your self-discipline it can be helpful to look inward and make a list of what you want to change and the items, settings or activities that trigger the negative behaviors you wish to change. While it can be difficult to confront yourself so bluntly all at once, looking at what you need to change will make it easier to establish ways to change it.

Practice makes perfect: If you feel that you will have an especially hard time deviating from a negative habit or routines, it can be helpful to try avoiding whatever it may be for a short period of time to allow yourself the opportunity to know what fully committing to a more self-disciplined lifestyle will be like thus allowing you to prepare for its effects beforehand. While a practice session can be beneficial, if you allow it to turn into several such sessions then you are just prolonging the negative habit.

Keep an eye out for triggers: When it comes to getting in the habit of practicing self-discipline, it is critical that you take the time early on to consider the types of things that commonly trigger you to lose control. Getting a better handle on your triggers will make it easier to understand the underlying habits they prop up, which will make it easier for you to avoid the whole affair in the future. While you might not be able to think of any triggers right away, if you keep the topic on your mind, then as you go through your week you should notice things that are more likely to stray from the chosen path.

Removing triggers: Once you have managed to make a list of your triggers, the next thing you are going to want to do is everything in your power to ensure you remove them from your general line of sight until you have your habit of being self-disciplined down pat. While you will rarely be able to remove absolutely all the power a given trigger has, you should be able to lessen it significantly, with practice. It is important to keep in mind that the early days are likely going to be tough going, but each time you withstand a serious temptation it will get a little easier.

Build a routine: Regardless of your self-discipline goals, if you aren't already maintaining a schedule where you can eat regularly, then it is important to make doing so a priority. Not only will eating at regular periods help you to feel better, but it will also ensure that your brain has the fuel required to make good decisions. Specifically, studies show that those with low blood sugar are three times more likely to make poor decisions based on a lack of resolve than those whose blood sugar was on point.

Scheduling (writing down a list): Perhaps the most important thing to do in taking control of your free time is to take stock of exactly how much you have and divide it up accordingly by writing it out. This might seem obvious, but I can't tell you how many people I know that just have their schedule inside their head and still expect to get everything done. People are prone to forget things, and I hate to break it to those of you who think you can reach maximum productivity this way, but I promise you, sooner or later you too will forget something you otherwise would've remembered had you written it down.

Mental Toughness Mindset

And no, you don't always need to keep a notepad and pencil on you, because you know that smartphone of yours? Yeah, the one that's either within arm's reach from you right now, or possibly the thing you're using to read this book with? Well, that thing isn't only a powerful tool to stay connected to the things and people you need connection with; it's also your very own personal assistant that can aid you in making great use of the free time you have so you can start making strides in what you want to accomplish.

All you need to do is open a blank document or list app every Sunday night – or before whichever day you want your week to start – and title it: To-Do This Week. Then, simply, write down what it is you want to accomplish that week.

- Exercise

- Start planning that trip

- Declutter the apartment and put some things on Craigslist

- Etc.

Don't make excuses: When you first set out to reach your goal, it is perfectly natural for your mind to start putting up roadblocks to all your new hard work in the form actions that are more immediately gratifying instead. While these alternatives might be gratifying in the short-term, they are not going to be nearly as satisfying in the long-term as succeeding at your dream of becoming famous would be.

It is important to understand that while it is easy to give into the short-term satisfaction now, you are sure to regret it later when the minor happiness from distraction dissipates and you are still no closer to achieving anything that will measurably increase the quality of your life as a whole. If you just can't seem to get your mind to fall in line, then you may find success with the concept of bargaining, which can help to keep things in check until your self-discipline has properly developed.

For example, if you feel as though you could be more physically fit but are having a hard time exercising as much as you know you should because you are constantly making excuses as to why you can't start your YouTube channel, then you can bargain with yourself to get yourself going and building positive habits. You could set up a reward system for yourself, and essentially train your brain the way you would a puppy. As time goes on, and you start to see serious results, then you won't need to use the bargaining system anymore as the results will speak for themselves.

If bargaining doesn't work, then you may find better success by making a concentrated effort to change the excuses that your mind is coming up with. Rather than telling yourself that it's okay and that you can always start tomorrow, get tough with yourself and blame the true source of the problem for the issues you are facing getting started.

Make a wholehearted commitment: One of the biggest keys to self-discipline is having a commitment to your goal. This gives you the biggest reason to keep pushing on if you can hold yourself accountable. If you can't then you will find that it is hard to hold on to your commitment, which can cause some problems.

You can make a personal commitment, or you can make a public commitment. While a public commitment may seem like it is the easiest to keep, that may not be the truth. Often, those around us may find themselves discouraging us from achieving our goals due to a feeling of inadequacy amongst themselves. It is much easier to keep a personal commitment because you will be able to build yourself up, rather than depending on others to build you up instead.

Committing yourself to your goal does not mean you will automatically succeed though. You must have a more detailed commitment than "I will get this done."

You must commit yourself not only to your goal, but to doing what it takes to achieve your goal and to finding the steps that you can take to make achieving your goal that much more possible. If you are not committing yourself fully, then you may not make your goal.

Commit yourself to consistency. You must be consistent in your daily habit changes to achieve your goal. If you lack consistency, it is so much easier to fall back into your old ways than it is to keep yourself moving towards your goal.

Critical Thinking Steps for Improved Self-Discipline

Problem Identification: Your first task in critical thinking is figuring out whether there is a problem at the current moment. At times, when you must figure this out, you might realize that there isn't an actual problem, only a simple mistake or misunderstanding going on. If you decide that there is a problem now, the next step is determining what the issue is. The ability to look at the positives and negatives and state and define the issue is a mark of high intelligence.

Analyzing the Issue: Next, you need to consider the issue from every angle possible. Can you solve this problem? Is it a concrete issue or mostly in our own mind? Can you do this on your own or will you be needing assistance from other people? At times, assessing the situation from various perspectives will lead to an easy and obvious resolution for the issue. In addition, it could help you realize your own biases in the situation.

List Possible Answers: Now, you should do some brainstorming and think of a few different solutions to the issue. There are many different answers for each problem. List any solution that you come up with and then try to narrow down each possibility at the end of this practice. When you have more than one possible solution, you increase your chances of finding the right one.

Choose a Solution: Next, you should select the solution that appears to apply best to this situation you're in. Various situations will require different answers to the issue. A lot of times, what will solve one situation, won't apply to another one that is similar. Figure out which will work for your current problem. Do this only after you have given this plenty of thought and can make an informed and intelligent decision on the matter.

Chapter 4:
Improve Your Attitude

People with low self-esteem tend to wallow in negativity. By focusing on the negative, you ignore large amounts of information that might otherwise make you feel better about yourself. Healthy self-esteem is the goal here. There is a sea of difference between, "I really need to be more physically active" than "I am a lazy blob." Excessive self-loathing can heavily backfire because it shifts the focus from ways through which one can improve on their failures.

Over a longer period, negative self-speak can up your stress level, and lead to major depression. Learning to tame negative self-talk is the key to overcoming challenges, feeling more confident and achieving the life of your dreams. If you have struggled with self-esteem for some time, chances are that you often overlook the positive aspects of your life. Positivity is powerful; this chapter will provide suggestions for harnessing its powers in order to go through life with better self-esteem.

Positive Self-Talk: Self-talk is the interactions that you have with the voice that resides inside of your own mind. The things that this voice says greatly affect the way that you feel and think. As such, negative self-talk can lead to saddening thought patterns and a lack of self-esteem. Consequently, positive self-talk is an essential component in building up one's self-esteem.

Making the practice of positive self-talk a regular habit should be your goal in terms of self-talk outcomes. Practicing positive self-talk might feel unusual or funny when you first begin, but, after you start to benefit from its self-esteem boosting effects, you will yearn for the opportunity to engage in positive self-talk uninterrupted.

Positive self-talk does not necessarily involve pointing out the things that you wish to change. For example, you might tell yourself that you want to behave less erratically, experience fewer feelings of anxiety, and stop living in a messy apartment. However, the problem with these thoughts lies in the fact that they focus on what you would rather not have. Instead, positive self-talk should focus on the things and outcomes that you do indeed want.

Positive self-talk takes place in the present-tense and affirms the qualities that correlate with high self-esteem. For example, repeat to yourself affirmations like "I am assertive," "I can make as much money as I want to," and "I feel calm."

Throw negative self-talk into a box: Visualize your mistakes in a tiny box the next time you find yourself exaggerating each of them. For instance, if you find yourself underperforming at a meeting or presentation, rather than thinking, it's the end of your career, try rationalizing by criticizing your choice of words. "I could have used better words, or my choice of words wasn't up to the mark." This really sounds more believable than "I screwed up my career." Visualize a small box and put your poor choice of words into it. You will subconsciously diminish the problem's size and end up feeling way more confident.

Practice possibility thinking: If you are constantly thinking in extremely glowing terms, you may trigger the mental lie detector which tells you that you are functioning in a surreal world. Do not force yourself to resort to extremely unreal positive thoughts. Instead, take a neutral approach when you are besieged with negative thoughts. Be more neutral in your thinking. Think about possibilities why a certain thing could have occurred. When you feel heavy and low on energy, instead of saying, "I am a fleshy seal or fat cow" or even, "I am a goddess or diva, irrespective of how I look" try saying, "I'd be really nice if I can knock off a few pounds. It will make me feel healthier, more energetic and fitter." We've taken a more middle and neutral ground here since changing negative to positive self-talk quickly can be highly unrealistic. Adopt a more realistic, practical and gradual approach.

Affirmations: Emotions that feed a negative attitude are triggered by the way you perceive situations that you have previously been in and those that are on the horizon. These perceptions are, in turn, influenced by the filters that your mind has built up over time based on the data it has recorded from the experiences you have had. When you find yourself thinking through this type of negative filter you will likely only see the negative aspects of a given situation, regardless of the positive ones that existed at the same time. If you chronically see every glass as half empty, then you may have an issue with negative filters.

In fact, if your attitude gets bad enough, your filters will likely go so far as to remove all of the calming and positive aspects of your day so all you can see are the things that make you unhappy, compounding the problem and making it seem as though there is no way to solve it. This is where affirmations and mantras come in as the repetition that comes along with them is a great way to bypass these filters and allow your mind to let in some new thoughts for a change.

An affirmation is simply a positive sentence that you write down multiple times throughout the day. A mantra is the same sentence, just repeated in your mind instead of written down. They are both a great way to quiet the mental background noise that is created by your anxiety and to eventually retrain your brain, bypassing the existing mental filters in the process.

- Examples include:
- *Today, you are perfect*
- *Forward progress! Just keep moving!*

- *You are the sky*

- *I am attracting all the love I dream of and deserve*

- *Follow my path to happiness*

- *I am strong. I am beautiful. I am enough*

- *I am grateful for my life so far and for what is to come*

- *I am fulfilled*

Consider core beliefs: If you have been dealing with a negative outlook for most of your life, then it is possible that there are facets of your core belief system that may ultimately end up being incompatible with the way the world works. The first step in getting past this issue is to determine the mental agreements that are coming into play so that you can correct them and move forward in a more effective fashion. These mental agreements often come in bundles which means if you can find the package of beliefs that are being affected, you will be on the right track.

As with many of the exercises discussed in this book, it can be difficult to get started with this exercise, but if you keep it up you will find that it gets much easier with practice. The best way to get started is going to be by working to uncover the core belief that is giving you the most trouble now. You can think of uncovering this core belief as solving a mystery which means you need to look for clues that are left in place by your subconscious.

Therefore, it is so important to distinguish these types of thoughts from actual core beliefs as your thoughts are rarely to be trusted if you are dealing with an extremely entrenched negative attitude. When it comes to tracking down a core belief now, the best way is to follow the trail of emotions you are having in response to an event. You will want to continue to question your specific emotions and the ways in which they are being externally influenced in order to get to the core beliefs that are pulling the strings.

Learn to properly manage rejection: It can be easy to get discouraged in the face of adversity, which is why it can be so effective to cognitively refrain the situation by putting the issue into perspective in the grand scheme of things. Most things are going to become infinitely unimportant over time which is why this can be such an effective strategy, especially for those things that really seem like they are the end of the world now. What's more, by looking at things for a more manageable angle you may even find a way to turn the issue around now that you previously hadn't considered.

Find the good in every situation: While you may have heard this advice before, rather than taking it as a general admonition to be positive you should think of it more as a thought exercise. Specifically, task yourself with finding something positive in every situation, regardless of how hopeless it might seem on the surface and then don't stop thinking about it until you have come up with a reason that holds at least a little water. If you can manage to find the good in situations that tax your mental and physical endurance to the ultimate test, then the rest should be easy.

One useful way of going about doing so is by finding the humor hiding in even the most trying and darkest situations. Try and crack a joke or, at the very least, remind yourself that it is sure to make a good story at some point in the future. Alternately, you can counter the grim prospect of the darkest timeline by putting an absurdist bent on the whole affair. For example, if you find out you are being laid off at the end of the week, then you can focus on figuring out the most absurd things you can do with your final days or the outlandish jobs you could pursue next.

Kriya: A kriya is a precise sequence of exercises that are used to reach a specific goal. The kriya for abdominal strength is a mixture of breathing exercises and precise movements that are designed to strengthen the core while also teaching you to find the internal strength required to turn your back on your bad habits. Furthermore, it is also known to power up the third chakra in a way that is commonly thought to serve as a starting point for future feelings of transformation and empowerment. Once you have finished this kriya, it is likely that you will feel more balanced, grounded and generally at one with the universe.

If you plan on starting off with this kriya then you are going to want to ensure you can commit to doing it every single day for 40 days. This is how long it will take for your brain to start forming the types of pathways that you should be aiming for as they will be free of the bad habits that you were previously cultivating.

You start this meditative exercise by lying on your back with your legs stretched out straight and your arms at your sides. You can also place them beneath your lower back if you need additional support in that area. Once you are in the position you will then want to inhale slowly while at the same time flexing your core while you slowly lift your right leg into the air until it is perpendicular to the floor. You are going to want to breathe in while getting into this position, hold it for a few seconds and then exhale as you slowly return it to the ground. You will then want to repeat the same steps for the other leg before repeating the process for a total of three minutes.

Chapter 5:
Improve Your Control of Negative Emotions

Cognitive Behavioral Therapy, more commonly known as CBT, is a type of therapy that works around the assumption that there are simply some behaviors that cannot be controlled through conscious thought alone. In fact, it posits that all behaviors occur thanks to a mixture of internal and external stimuli and a lifetime of conditioning in one an infinite number of ways.

While it was first created to help those with depression deal with their condition, this type of psychotherapy has become a popular way of dealing with a wide variety of issues including anger and anxiety as well. At its heart, however, its primary goal is to help users mitigate problems they are having directly by finding their associated negative behaviors and any associated thoughts and then changing them into something more beneficial. CBT is a mixture of behavioral therapy and cognitive therapy and thus makes use of the guiding principles of each.

While the techniques discussed in this will be more effective if you work on them with a therapist who specializes in CBT, you can also find success if you stick with them yourself. When you first begin attempting CBT techniques it is vital that you remember that you are developing a new skill as well. What this means is that, just like any other skill, you are going to have a difficult time of things at first but that things will get easier each day if you keep it up and don't get discouraged. While this is easy to say, it is important to take it to heart as the first time you try many of the exercises in the following chapter you may very well fail which is why having unrealistic expectations up front can make it easier to get back on the horse should the situation arise.

Breathe properly: In many stressful situations, if the mind is feeling overwhelmed, the first thing the body does is alter its breathing. The way you are breathing is essentially the trigger that directly affects everything else the way your body functions. When you receive either to little or too much oxygen it serves to significantly enhance the seriousness of any other symptoms that might be present, making a mild issue into a serious attack in no time flat.

Luckily, learning to control your breathing can be quite straightforward as soon as you start actively thinking about it. The quickest means of doing so is via what is known as the 4/7/8 method. To practice this method all you need to do is find a comfortable place to sit, sit with your shoulders square and your back straight and then breathe in slowly for a total of four seconds. Next, you will want to hold your breath for a total of seven seconds and then breathe out slowly for a total of eight seconds. You will want to repeat this process until the issue resolves itself or you have completed six repetitions for a total of two minutes. You may want to close your eyes as well, to help yourself relax even more.

While you might not notice much of a change at first, over time you will find that when you do this exercise that everything around you begins to slow down, taking your heartbeat with it. If two minutes doesn't seem to be enough for you, then you may want to work up to five minute sessions, or even 10, the important thing is that you find the right amount of focused breathing that works for you so you can bust it out when you need it most.

Progressive muscle relaxation: Progressive muscle relaxation is a technique, like measured breathing, that can be used now to deal with particularly bad anxiety flair ups. It involves tensing and then relaxing specific groups of muscles as a means of distracting your anxiety and short circuiting the loop that causes it to manifest in the first place. This is since it is difficult for your body to maintain a tensed, anxious state, and a relaxed calm state at the same time. As such, if you feel an anxiety attack coming your way, a period of focused relaxation may be just what you need to cut it off at the pass. You may also find this type of exercise useful if you are having difficulty sleeping.

While you will eventually be able to use this exercise now, while you are still getting the hang of it you are going to want to find some place quiet where you can focus on the task at hand. Give yourself 15 to 20 minutes of practice time to start, though once you get the hang of it you will likely be able to experience the same results in far less time. To start, you simply need to pick a specific part of your body and shift the entirety of your focus to it. This step will be the same regardless of which muscle group you are focusing on.

After you have finished tensing, you will then want to abruptly change course and relax the muscles you were focusing on (in this case your hand). After you have finished tensing you will want to relax those muscles completely, feeling all the tightness float out of your muscles, and from your mental state as well. You will want to go completely limp for this exercise to be effective, before then focusing on the difference between the two states.

Journaling: Your thoughts are a continuous stream; there are no waking moments where you aren't thinking about something. It may not also be in the front of your mind, but thoughts are always present and always moving. As the adage goes, "I think, therefore I am." It's difficult to recognize everything that passes through our heads as it is. Throw anxiety into the mix and it becomes impossible to follow everything.

A journal is a great way to track your anxiety. By putting your thoughts on paper you'll give them tangible form. Though like a diary, an anxiety journal isn't for just a record of your daily happenings. It's closer to an operating table where you'll examine, dissect, and explore your distressing thoughts. This is helpful in several ways:

Better self-expression. How often have you tried to explain your anxiety to someone only to feel like they didn't fully understand what you were saying? It's difficult to articulate worry, especially now. But no one will have a better understanding of your thought processes than you do. By laying it out on the page you can practice how you can communicate it to others. In therapy sessions, you can even read your entries to your therapist.

Self-reflection. As we become more aware of ourselves and our thought cycles it can become easy to let thoughts get lost in the blur. If you have a written record of your thoughts it acts likes a map of sorts. You can see what sort of thoughts you had on any given day and see how they changed overtime, creating pathways and patterns that you can recognize overtime. This recognition will help you develop plans going forward.

Progress. It's also beneficial to have the journal of your thoughts because it shows how much progress you make on your journey to recovery. But of equal value to these positives are seeing where you come up short. You are going to want to use the ABCD model for describing your experiences.

First, you will list the activating event, including an explanation of the situation, with all personal bias removed, this should just state the facts. You will also want to make note of the first thing crossed your mind when the event occurred as this is likely an automatic thought which means knowing it could be useful later. From there, you will want to write down any beliefs that came into play as well, starting with the type of negative thoughts you experienced. If possible, you are also going to want to write down the source of the belief as well.

From there, you are going to want to write down the relevant consequences that occurred from the way you handled the incident, both short and long-term. Finally, if possible, you are going to want to dispute your negative thoughts and replace them with alternatives that you could have used instead. It is important to get into the habit of writing in your journal at the end of every single day.

When dealing with CBT, it is impossible to have too much information about what is going on in your daily life, the more events you write down each day the better. While initially, you may have a difficult time remembering the finer details of the things that happen to you throughout the day, it is important to keep up the practice regardless.

Self-soothing: If you find yourself in a situation with a trigger that you simply cannot abide, and your only option seems to be having a panic or anxiety attack, then you may find it useful to distract yourself with alternative stimuli in order to short circuit the attack and help yourself self-correct. The specifics of what you do to take yourself out of the moment doesn't matter, if it serves to take your mind off the negative emotion that is threatening to spill out.

You can start by doing something as simple as paying attention to what is around you, finding a calm spot to be by yourself temporarily, or even find something shiny to keep yourself entertained until the feeling passes. You may also find listening to music to be effective, getting a massage or even literally stopping to smell the roses.

Finding something salty or sugary to eat will also give you a caloric boost that will often serve to get your mind on the right track.

Radical acceptance: Radical acceptance is a healthy alternative to many habitual avoidance techniques that you can use when you come across a situation that, at face value, seems extremely unfair or otherwise completely out of your control. Rather than focusing on this injustice now, you can instead practice accepting the negative situation as a fact and instead focusing your mental efforts on doing everything you can to solve the problem at hand.

It is important to keep in mind that there is a clear difference between accepting something and agreeing or approving of the way in which it is proceeding. Acceptance is the best solution when a situation seems completely beyond your control; for example, if you find out that you did not get the promotion that you were hoping for, an unhealthy, but extremely common, the response is to blame your superiors for their shortsightedness.

Exercise More

Several studies prove that exercise is an effective way to fight negative emotions and other mental disorders like depression, anxiety, and phobias. Exercise can help relieve stress, improves overall mood, improves memory, and increase the amount of quality sleep you get each night. Perspiration releases natural endorphins which are the hormones that make us feel happy and positive. If you haven't exercised in a while, the following set of exercises should allow you to choose a level that's right for you.

10-minute-high intensity workout: You will want to complete the entire circuit three times and take a 10 second rest between each set. Each circuit should take 3 minutes and 10 seconds.

Sumo squats: Start with your feet at slightly more than hip-width apart and keep your toes pointed facing outward at a 45-degree angle. Place all your weight on the heels of your feet, your chest upright and your back straight, lower yourself down towards the ground until your thighs are essentially parallel to the ground. Using your quads and your glutes, push yourself back into the starting position. To end each set, move into a reverse lung and fold your body forward while keeping your arms stretched overhead.

Jumping jacks: Start by standing in a relaxed stance, with your feed about hip-width apart and your arms resting at your sides. Jump up while spreading your feet and raising your arms above your head. Repeat as many times as possible, as quickly as possible, for about 45 seconds.

Jab, cross, front kick (left): Start with your left foot in front of your right foot and your hips facing right. Raise your arms so that you are in somewhat of a boxer stance. Start with a jab by punching forward with your left arm straight out. Move directly into throwing a cross by punching with your left arm and rotating your body to the right.

Stephen Patterson

Chapter 6:
Improve Your Leadership Skills

It is easy to lead; it is difficult to lead well. If you are interested in leading others to the best of their abilities, make sure you strive to always embody the following traits.

Be aware: A good leader understands that there are some inalienable differences between the rank-in-file, middle and senior management, accepts this as fact and acts accordingly. It is important to be aware of how you interact with your team and to always conduct yourself in a way that doesn't suggest superiority but simply allows you to retain an unbiased perspective. This can be a difficult quality to master as it is most people's first impulse to make friends with the people they work with. This will ultimately lead to disaster however as there will always come a time when the leader must be a leader and not a friend. Cut this inevitable paradox off at the pass, treat your team well but make sure it is clear where your loyalties lie.

Be decisive: Being a leader means making the sorts of decisions that other folks don't want to make. Being the sort of leader that separates themselves from the crowd means accepting this fact and seeing every decision you make through to the end. This doesn't mean to make all decisions in a vacuum; however, a good leader knows when it is time to gather input and when it is time to act. A leader who is known to be decisive will be supported by their team when they must make quick decisions as they will have a history of quality decisions to back them up.

Be empathetic: One part of being a leader than many people struggle with is giving criticism when it is due. Having empathy for the people you are responsible for does not mean avoiding criticism or always giving in to their requests; rather, it means taking their feelings into account and dealing with issues appropriately.

Help your team to grow as individuals: Your team is only as strong as its weakest member which is why it is important to encourage your team to grow under your leadership. You can ensure this is the case by taking the time to get to know each member of your team and their specific strengths and weaknesses. Take the time to provide them with leadership opportunities of their own and to find ways to help them shine while improving the team at the same time. Everyone has something unique to offer the group, a good leader can determine what that is and help nourish it for the good of the whole.

Follow your own example: If you want your team to arrive early, work late, always be prepared and work as hard as possible you need to be willing to go the extra mile with them. A leader who preaches hard work and sacrifice but commits to neither is not the sort of leader that a team will follow for any reasonable period. Sometimes being the leader means towing a difficult party line thrown down by someone higher in the chain of command, your team will take difficult changes much better if they know you are with them in practice and not just in spirit.

This goes for positive changes as well as negative ones. Your team will follow your lead, if you want to have a more open collaborative workspace, get your team involved. If you want them to take more initiative, make the decision to let them make their own decisions. Do as I say and not as I do may work when dealing with children, but your team will spot any hypocrisy and It will poison your relationship with them permanently. Stick to uniformity when it comes to which rules apply to whom and you will be much happier in the long run.

Consider Your Body Language

Show them you are the leader: It is important that you try to project as strong and powerful of body language cues as possible when around your team to help you appear to be as full of leadership material as possible. This will help you seem more trustworthy as well as more competent, two things that are especially important for a new leader to possess. Even better, acting this way will help you feel both more in control of the situation which will make you better equipped to handle the task you have been given. It is important to not be so authoritative that you lose the ability to speak with your team in a tacit fashion.

Be aware of your stature: Having the right stature is about more than standing the right way and stopping yourself from slouching, though this is extremely important as well. A good leader is never tired and always willing to go the extra mile for their team. If you want to have the stature of a leader you are going to want to modify your nonverbal cues to ensure you project the types of cues, you expect a leader to project whenever you are with your team. This doesn't mean that you always must have all the answer and a clear grasp of what is coming next, it just means your team needs to feel that they are being led in a competent fashion.

Don't get to close: A good leader has the respect of their team, but always remains apart from them as well. This means you need to give off the nonverbal cues to ensure they know they can talk to you but keep enough of a distance that they don't feel as though they can question you when things get rough. It can be a difficult line to walk but it is crucial to do so if you hope to be an effective leader.

Watch for barriers: Other important body languages to be on the lookout for includes anything that generates a physical barrier. Common examples of this are crossed arms or holding documents or other props in hand and pressed tightly to the chest. These are all signs that the other person is not receptive to what the other person is saying. In fact, one study looked at more than 2,000 negotiations take place and none of them ended in success if one member never uncrossed their arms.

These behaviors show that the person in question is either emotionally or mentally blocked off from whatever is going on in front of them. This is an unintentional habit which is what makes it so useful when it comes to getting to the heart of the matter. Likewise, if a person starts off using this type of body language, and then changes their tune, you will know that you have managed to win them over to your side.

Copycat: When discussing something important with another person, the easiest way to tell if you are winning them over to your side is if you catch them copying your body language. It could be something as simple as a hand gesture or crossing or uncrossing your legs, the specific action doesn't matter all that matters is that it happened at all. If the other person starts mimicking the things you do, then you know that whatever argument you are using is working.

An interesting fact is that this type of copycat behavior is not only indicative of what the other person is currently thinking, it can also influence opinions as well. As such, if you can get the other person to start copying your movements, you can make it more likely that they are going to start agreeing with you as well. In order to set up this type of scenario, you will want to start by subtly copying the things the other person does.

Fake it: Specifically, you may find that faking a degree of confidence in your leadership skills that you don't yet feel can be an extremely effective way to improve social interactions of all types, without having to have fully deal with the issues that may be at the root of your lack of confidence. While this might sound ridiculous, take a moment and consider a scenario where you were interacting with a person who you identify as being supremely confident. Now consider all the things about this person that made you believe they were confident and ask yourself how would you have known if they were faking it?

The truth of the matter is that if you act confidently in each situation then those around you will have no reason to assume you feel otherwise. As such, pretending to have confidence and being confident are two sides of the same coin. What's more, having success when pretending to have confidence once, will make it much easier to do a second time, and what's more, each additional time you pretend to have confidence you will have to pretend less and less until you won't be pretending at all.

In order to act the way a confident person would act in each situation; all you need to do is to visualize someone you know who is confident and then ask yourself what they would do if they were in your position. From there, it is just a matter of following their lead. Think about the way they would present themselves, what type of gestures they would use, what type of body language they would utilize and how they would speak. With a good role model to follow you will be surprised at how easy playing pretend can be.

Incremental improvement: One of the major duties of an effective leader is to constantly evaluate different aspects of the team in order to ensure it is operating at peak efficiency. The leader will also need to keep up to date on customer requirements as this is something that is going to be constantly changing as well. Doing so is one of the only truly reliable ways of staying ahead of the curve by making it possible to streamline the overall direction of the team towards the processes that will achieve the best results.

In order to ensure that this is the case, an effective leader will want to make time in their schedule to look at the results and then compare them to the costs as a means of discovering the best ways to use all the resources available to them at the given time. This will include things like evaluating the organization in hopes of making it more efficient and reliable.

Stephen Patterson

Chapter 7:
Improve Your Emotional Intelligence

Emotional Intelligence (or, EQ) is "the ability to identify and manage your own emotions and the emotions of others." This includes three skills:

- Emotional awareness

- The ability to harness and apply emotions to tasks

- The ability to manage emotions

While it may seem like a simple concept, the truth is not many people are very high in Emotional Intelligence. How would someone even know if they were Emotionally Intelligent and, more importantly, how it might be affecting their life?

There are so many theories on Emotional Intelligence, why it's important and how it can be used. However, there are a few key elements to EQ that seem to be found in every discussion. The first, and arguably most important, element is self-awareness since without knowing and understanding yourself, your own emotions, your triggers, etc., how can you perform any self-assessment to grow or improve? Correctly identifying your own emotions is the basis for EQ.

Self-regulation comes from self-awareness. Once you are in sync with your own emotions and understand when and why you feel them, you can then regulate them. In other words, if you know that you get very angry when someone talks down to you, you can prepare yourself to preemptively disrupt your anger.

Thinking before acting is key in controlling emotions as well as withholding judgement of others. Most people tend to react in emotionally intense situations, having angry outbursts when something goes wrong or taking constructive criticism personally to the point of becoming depressed. People also tend to judge others before trying to understand why that person is saying, doing or feeling something. Self-regulation allows you to put yourself in another's shoes which allows for a positive emotional response as opposed to a careless reaction.

EQ Is Not for The Lazy.

When it comes to your day to day interactions with others, empathy is hands-down one of the most valuable elements of emotional intelligence. While it is often confused with either compassion or sympathy, empathy is the ability to understand and relate to the emotions of another person. It directly relates back to withholding judgement, which is reinforced through self-regulation. Those who have a high degree of empathy can understand when others are feeling a specific way and respond according to their goals and desires.

For example, if someone is depressed because they didn't get a promotion, the empath will try to cheer that person up and redirect them from the depressed state even if they don't much care one way or the other. Empathy is the difference between listening to what someone is saying and understanding what they are feeling.

Those with naturally high EQ are often leaders because they have a natural ability to connect with others, manage their emotions and inspire them in one way or another. This is often a natural result of the other elements of emotional intelligence and it is possible the leader in question isn't even doing such things intentionally, their situation is just a result of their innate abilities.

Getting Started

If you feel as though your EQ may not be where you want it to be, there are several simple exercises you can start with to help you move in the right direction. You are going to want to practice the following at least twice a day, once in the morning and once at night to keep you in an emotionally intelligent mindset. When choosing the time to start your exercises, ensure that it is a time you can easily repeat each day as your mind will take to the practice more easily with the added repetition. Finally, you will want to practice each day for a full month in order to ensure these exercises become full-blown habits.

Practice Active Listening: During arguments or disagreements, we often listen not to understand but to react and respond. When the other person is speaking, we are almost mentally constructing out own arguments to answer back or give back to them. This leads to even more conflict.

Dealing with conflict becomes more effective when you tackle issues in an assertive yet respective manner, without being defensive. When you listen empathetically, your own thoughts and emotions are considered. Listening actively and empathetically can help you shed toxic feelings building up in you.

Be assertive, but also practice active listening to find that one point that can lead to a resolution. Problem solution only happens when you understand where the other person is coming from and what they want. You can find a middle ground only when you tune in to the words, feelings, and emotions of the other person, not just to give a fitting reply but also to resolve the issue. Listening is all about putting the other person's words, thoughts, and feelings first.

Your opinion about people or events may not change. However, the time spent listening to the other person may just calm you and help you come up with a more positive or constructive response. It may help you see things from a different perspective and analyze the situation more objectively.

Practice being more lighthearted: When you are more lighthearted and optimistic, it is simpler to capture the goodness of everyday situations and objects. Positivity results in greater emotional happiness and increased opportunities. People are forever looking to be around optimistic folks who come up with positive connections and possibilities. When you become more negative, you only concentrate on what can go awry rather than building strong resistance.

People with a more evolved emotional quotient know how to utilize wit and humor to make everyone feel happier, positive and safer. They know the art of using laugher to tide over tough times.

Learn to take note of how you are feeling: For most people, each day is a jumble of appointments and deadlines that make it difficult to find an extra moment to breathe, much less take stock of their emotional state. Unfortunately, getting into this mindset will make it much easier for actions to slip through subconsciously that are a response to the emotional state in question. Therefore, it is important to practice communicating with yourself and prioritize those communications when they do occur.

Emotions are often tied to events that are currently taking place in your immediate surroundings, but unfortunately, that doesn't mean the emotion is a valid response to the events. The emotion might instead be tied to a previous event that the current situation is simply recalling. If this is the case, while the emotion might feel totally real to you, it is in no way relevant to the scenario in question. Learning to understand which emotions you are feeling and why is an important step towards improving your EQ.

Being aware of your feelings is a skill which means that like any other skill it will only improve with practice. As such, it is important to pick a specific time every morning and every evening where you can check-in on your feelings and determine the root cause of whatever you find. This should be a pair of relatively busy points so that the odds of you experiencing a relatively complex emotion is somewhat high for the best effect. Consider the physical response the emotion is eliciting and how it makes you feel and make sure you connect it to a specific emotion and find that emotion's source.

Figure out what triggers the emotion. Everyone has a trigger when it comes to their emotions. It is not random when you get mad and explode at the people around you. If you want to start working on your emotional intelligence and get it to work for you, it is important that you learn what some of these triggers are all about.

For many people, the triggers that come with anger would include something that stress or insecurities. When they are dealing with a lot of stress at work or home or elsewhere, they are more likely to lash out at even the smallest thing. But is it worth harming other people and making them feel bad because you are a little bit stressed out about something? Learning how to properly manage your stress levels and keep them low is one of the best things that you can do in this situation.

If it is your insecurities that are causing issues, you may need to work on whatever is causing that in your life. Just because someone says something or constructively critiques you at work doesn't mean that you can just blow up and act in a violent or horrible way. Learning how to deal with these insecurities, or even what is causing those insecurities, can make a big difference in how you will react to others.

There are many triggers that can cause you to act out when your emotions are started. But you must be the one who is in control of those emotions, no matter what. Learning what those triggers are and taking care of them as quickly as possible will ensure that you will be able to control your emotions instead of letting them take over your life.

Own up to your actions: Accepting complete responsibility for your actions is one of the first steps towards developing higher emotional quotient. People who are emotionally intelligent don't feel the need to shift responsibility on someone else, justify their wrongdoings or defend themselves aggressively. They shy away from putting the blame elsewhere and completely own up to the mistake.

On the contrary, they accept responsibility for their actions and learn important lessons from it. Unlike people low on emotional intelligence or self-esteem, they do not ascribe their mistakes to external circumstances or factors that are supposedly outside their control. They accept their choices, bad decisions and less than perfect actions.

When you accept your mistakes, it is easier to control, be responsible for and manage your feelings and behavior in the future. Blaming the situation or another person only takes away from helping you control the situation more effectively moving ahead. It also helps you gain a perspective about your own abilities and weaknesses. When acknowledging that something went wrong as a result of your choices and decisions, you are in a more gainful position to tackle it.

You acquire the ability to control your emotions, manage negative feelings, develop more fruitful interpersonal relationships, wield better decisions and influencer your actions more positively. You are not replying on others or external circumstances for determining your emotions but taking charge of how you feel.

Tap into your inner passions: Everyone goes about their daily routine and work in a mechanical manner. However, there's always something that excites you or triggers your passion? What is it that you're most upbeat about doing? To move out of the rut, and gain more emotional stability or greater peace, take up a pursuit you are passionate about. This will lower your stress levels, release feel good chemicals in the brain, and increase your ability to handle emotions more effectively. When you are less stressed, it is easier to be in control of your feelings.

Manage your stress and anxiety: Stress and anxiety are your worst friends when you are trying to get a handle on your emotions. They will leave you feeling on edge and it won't take much for someone to push you over. Our modern day lives have made it easy to feel stressed out on a regular basis. From work to school to taking care of kids and more, it is a miracle that any of us can keep up with it all. Luckily, there are a lot of great options that you can choose from to help relieve the stress and make yourself feel better.

There are so many ways that you can work on your own stress and anxiety and the method that you use may include one of the other options that we have discussed in this guidebook. For example, a lot of people like to journal out their feelings and frustrations, and this can be a great way to increase your self-awareness as well. You may decide to go out on a walk to help reduce the impact of your emotions, so you don't react right away. Some people like to pick up a hobby, talk out their emotions with a friend, take a relaxing bath, or do something else that helps them get rid of the stress and feel so much better.

Picking out a method that helps you manage your stress and anxiety is so important. If you are feeling stressed and anxious all the time, it is going to be hard for you to concentrate on keeping those emotions in check. Find the stress reliever that works for you and make sure to keep it on hand whenever you may need it.

Chapter 8:
Improve Your Ability to Remain in Control

When it comes to remaining in control of your situation no matter what, the first thing you need to understand is that there is a difference between being in control and never being spontaneous. Instead, those who are truly in control always can remain aware of their situation and their personal state so that they can course correct at any point things stop going according to plan. Learning to be in control always means understanding your strengths and weakness as well as what can be done in any given situation to maximize the one while minimizing the other. Learning to take control of any situation will help you to master your emotions and ultimately live the type of life you have always dreamed of.

Controlling the current situation: If you find yourself in a situation that is rapidly spiraling out of control, the first thing you are going to want to do is to take a moment to calm yourself. If you are too distraught over whatever it is that is currently going on, then you will find it much more difficult to think clearly and critically about the situation you find yourself in. You may find that the breathing and relaxation exercises discussed in Chapter 5 are a big help when it comes to quickly and effectively calming yourself now.

With this out of the way, the next thing to do is to take stock of what you need to do first in order to start getting the situation under control. While it is important to plan, if possible, there is a chance you will need to take care of the most pressing issues first before taking the time to consider what the best course of action might be moving forward. When you do find the time to start planning it is important to ensure that you don't let your emotions or insignificant details distract you from what matters most.

If you are dealing with the current situation alone, you will find that sketching out a general plan of attack will help to immediately make you feel as though you are more in control of the current situation and thus ready to face whatever might be coming next. If you are with a group, the first person who can assess the situation and put together a plan that makes sense is likely going to be the one that everyone else falls in line behind.

When it comes to creating a plan in the moment, it is important to understand that you don't need to have absolutely all the details worked out beforehand, as long as you take the details you do have and work out the most logical course of action based on the specifics of those details. When looking to take control of a situation in the moment, if you wait until you have all the relevant details before you make a move then you risk being too late to the party and either not being able to do anything meaningful to move the situation towards your desired resolution or having to follow someone else's lead while they take charge instead.

Additionally, you may find that you have more confidence moving forward if you take a second to consider what variables you can control in the current situation. For example, if you are planning an event that will be taking place outdoors then it is impossible to control the weather but if it starts raining in the moment then you can do what you can to change the location or look for a means of keeping the current location dry.

When you are first getting used to taking charge in these types of situations, it is only natural to feel hesitant before speaking up, especially if this will lead to you overseeing a group of relative strangers. Therefore, it is important to take the immediate reaction that is required without hesitation so that you can do the right thing without worrying about getting waylaid by thoughts of doubt. While this will no doubt seem like a harrowing proposition at first, once you have leapt into action a few times you will find that the thought of doing so becomes far more manageable.

If you find yourself the person most prepared to lead others in an urgent situation then it is important that you speak in a commanding tone that expresses the fact that you have things under control. When it comes to explaining your plan to a group it is important that you don't push to get your own way and instead let the others decide what to do with the path you have provided them. Not forcing the issues shows that you are confident in the details you have set forth and means that anyone who doesn't like what you have to say will have to come up with a superior alternative.

An important part of taking charge of a given situation in the moment is the effective delegation of duties. Making sure that everyone has a part to play that suits their abilities requires not only an understanding of the situation, but an ability to understand what the strengths and weaknesses of others are. This goes for yourself as well, if you know that your leadership skills are not up to the task then there is no harm in putting forth your plan and then delegating the role of carrying it out to someone else. Getting through an urgent situation successfully means putting your personal feelings aside and doing what needs to be done in order to ensure success.

Controlling internal situations: When it comes to controlling any type of emotional turmoil you might be feeling, the first thing you will want to keep in mind is that it is important to not bottle up your emotions and instead to always really feel whatever it is that you are feeling. Welcoming your emotions and accepting them is the only way to truly understand them and thus control them effectively. Repressing your emotions doesn't mean you are in control it means you are letting them control you. suppressing your feelings in the long-term can lead to a wide variety of health problems including things like chronic pain, insomnia, and even heart disease.

The first thing you are going to want to do when it comes to ensuring you can properly control your emotions is always to keep a small journal with you that you can log your feelings in. This will make it easier for you to find out what is leading up to each outburst of feeling as well as your response to the emotion and how that response made you feel after the fact. This should make it possible for you to keep track of your triggers for various emotions, which is the first step to limiting them in a meaningful way.

You may also find it helpful if you take the extra step of giving your own painful memories that just won't leave you alone, longstanding insecurities or any other reoccurring bad thoughts you have your own unique name. For example, if you find yourself getting angry when someone cuts you off in traffic, not just annoyed but bordering on physical violence, then simply owing it as road rage can be surprisingly effective. The fact of the matter is that names have power, not only will naming these types of thoughts and feelings makes it easier for you to pinpoint when they are causing you to act irrationally, it will also give you some control over it as well.

Mental Toughness Mindset

Giving something a name is important because it also gives whatever is being named clear definition and context. Without a name, the feeling is just something nebulous that takes control when and where it wants to. Once it has a name it can be prepared against and ultimately controlled. When you feel the named feeling or thought coming on you can greet it by name and prepare yourself for what's coming next which should help you get some distance on things overall, thus preventing the negative thought or feeling from taking hold.

If you find that you lose control when certain thoughts or memories occur to you then this is likely because you are holding onto longstanding resentment, grudges, and anger. Making a conscious effort to forgive those who have betrayed you and feel compassion for those that have harmed you will not only make it easier to deal with any related thoughts or memories, it will also make you more resilient in the future because you have learned to keep your negative feelings under control.

Finally, if you find that your emotions are still more in control than you might like, then you might find talking to a professional to be a useful way to right whatever issues might be overtaking you. You may find that regularly talking to someone can help you come to terms with the patterns you fall into most often and, more importantly, learn new and improved responses to ensure you don't keep making the same mistakes time and again.

Take control in the long-term. Even if you can take control of a situation in the moment, you may still find it difficult to get things together enough to properly plan for the future. If this is the case, then you may find that simply taking stock of your issues will help you get back on track. It doesn't matter what issues you are dealing with, if you write them all down in order of importance then by the end you are sure to see that many are more manageable than you first expected.

If you find that you are having trouble getting started, then you are likely putting up too many mental filters. To get past them all you need to do is to set a timer for five minutes and then write down anything and everything that comes to mind until the timer goes off. While many of the things that you write likely won't make the cut upon closer consideration, you will almost surely come up with enough useful material to move forward with.

When making your list it is important to be as specific as possible and to also be honest with yourself as the only person you will hurt by lying is yourself. If you find that you still can't get past your mental filters, then you may want to get an outside perspective instead. You could try asking a friend or loved one for their opinions and use their observations to get your own creative juices flowing.

Once you have a good list to work from, the next step towards controlling your future is to set goals that will make your list come true. The specifics of setting appropriate goals is discussed in detail in chapter 12. Once you have your goals in mind, in order to ensure you control the outcome as much as possible it is important to utilize a technique known as mental contrasting. Mental contrasting involves looking at a specific task and then considering all the potential obstacles that could potentially get in the way of its completion. All you need to do is to take a few minutes to think about what could go wrong and what you can do in order to ensure that this is not the case.

Stephen Patterson

When it comes to dealing with tasks that involve other people it is important to set clear boundaries as to what is and is not acceptable and then stick to them. Likewise, it is important to respect boundaries that others set. It doesn't matter how healthy the relationship is, it should still have boundaries. It is also important to remain on the lookout for emotional manipulation as this can easily derail an otherwise promising plan in unexpected ways.

In addition to taking care of your mental health, it is important to take care of your physical health as well. This includes things like getting enough sleep each night and eating right. Remember, if you aren't taking the time to properly take control of your physical, mental, and emotional health then you can't always be in control.

Chapter 9:
Improve Your Ability to Trust Your Instincts

Conventional wisdom points out the importance of trusting one's gut but then gives very little guidance as to how to go about doing so. This type of gut instinct, also known as intuition, has to do with a person's innate understanding of a situation. It doesn't require additional research or follow up; it is just something you know. Intuition often arises as a type of feeling in the body that is unique to each person but odds are you have felt it from time to time when you knew deep down in your bones that, whatever you were doing at the time, you were on the right track.

Learning to listen to what your intuition has to say can make it easier to avoid potentially dangerous situations or potentially unhealthy relationships. Throughout your life, you will find many people have plans and ideas about your future, some with your best interests in mind and others not so much. It can often be difficult to tell what category a specific person falls into, but if you put aside all those external thoughts and opinions and list to your intuition instead then it is more likely to point you in the right direction.

Unfortunately, trusting your gut isn't something you can simply make the decision to do, it is a skill which means that much like any other skill it will only improve with practice. Luckily, even if you have never relied on your intuition before, it is still a part of you which means you can still reach it if you try. The following tips will help you start to draw it out more regularly in your day to day life.

Consider the things that get in the way: Your intuition acts much like the North Start which means that, if you aren't vigilant, things can get in the way of it telling you where to go next. Once you become aware of these obstructions, however, you'll find that it becomes much easier to tell when you are heading towards them and course correct accordingly.

One of the most common obstructions is overthinking which is the opposite of letting intuition guide you. Intuition is all about instinct, and if you spend too much time thinking and not enough time acting them you will find that you can't tune in to whatever it is your intuition is trying to get you to do. While planning is an important part of being successful in many instances, putting too much thought into a decision can make it difficult to ever actually get anything done.

If you find yourself stuck in this type of situation then it is likely that your thought process is being blocked or is working hard to build a case for the opposite decision compared to the one you just made up your mind about. This is known as analysis paralysis and it occurs when there are too many possible variables to make the process of making a choice manageable.

Another consequence of overthinking is an influx of considerations outlining why a specific course of action should have been taken as opposed to the one you decided on or why a course of action you are considering is almost guaranteed to go wrong. In these types of situations, you will often find that you are basing your presumed behavior based on what others expect, prefer, or think, as opposed to how you feel in the moment. This type of "should" thinking shifts the focus from internal to external, thus decreasing your ability to access your intuition.

Even though both unconscious biases and prejudices are essentially the opposite of overthinking a given scenario, they still have the same overall effect on your intuition. These sorts of biases serve to cause you to operate based on quick judgements that the brain automatically spits out based on what it believes it has learned from past experiences, regardless of whether these past experiences are true. As a result, they bypass any type of rational thought, making it impossible for you to tap into your intuition to determine the true course of action.

Accept your intuition: Another reason that many people have a hard time utilizing their intuition to its full effect is that accepting your intuition means listening to what it has to tell you, even when what it has to tell you isn't what you want to hear. Likewise, as it isn't a physical, or well-defined, sensation, it can be easy to brush it off, especially when it is telling you to do something that goes contrary to your regular nature.

For example, if you usually take a shortcut home from the bus stop through an alley but feel a tug in the back of your mind saying you should find another way home, you may want to ignore that fear as taking the long way around would add 20 minutes to your walk and you are tired after a long day. If you know enough to trust your intuition, however, then you would nevertheless make the trade off and find yourself feeling better about the trip almost immediately. Before you can trust your gut for good, however, you need to welcome intuition into your life, even if it doesn't always make sense, while at the same time making a commitment to it that you will follow where it leads.

Grow your intuition in the right way: After you have opened yourself up to the idea of being more receptive to your intuition, the next thing you will need to work on is experiencing it to the fullest. To do so successfully, you are going to want to find a quiet place where you can tune out the stress and distractions of your daily life. If you are rarely all by yourself then you may want to prepare yourself mentally for the change as it can be pretty jarring as you will be faced with all sides of yourself in a way that can be a bit intense for some people.

You may find that hidden emotions emerge from your mental depths and that you have issues to resolve that you previously weren't aware of. This is nothing to worry about, however, and is, indeed, all part of the process. This is also a key step as when you are truly alone you won't have anyone telling you what to do or what to think, you will be able to listen to yourself and see what your intuition has to say.

This will also allow you to clear your mind and slow down which can make it easier to break free of the haze most people find themselves in most of the time. It doesn't matter if you are physically or mentally tired, either way, it means you end up being at less than your best which makes it easier to miss information your intuition has been trying to tell you. Slowing own will also help you to better process and recognize the information you do receive in your mind and body.

This means you must push away the physical and mental clutter surrounding you by doing what you can in order to remove the greatest sense of urgency from the situation whether this is pushing back an upcoming deadline or physically stepping away from the situation either mentally or physically until you are free to finally listen to whatever it is that your intuition has been trying to tell you.

On the other hand, slowing down means taking deliberate actions to find space for your intuition to occupy. Sticking with a slower pace makes it easier to shift your perspective and clear away excess distractions so that you can feel and see the things that your intuition says matter the most. If you find it hard to physically get away from the issues that you are dealing with then mindfulness meditation, discussed in detail in the next chapter, could help as well.

Focus on yourself: Focusing on yourself can be as simple as looking inward to determine what you need to do in order to be successful in the current situation. This is a rare time where it is perfectly fine to make everything all about you which means you may need to give yourself permission to do so beforehand. If you find yourself shifting back to focusing on the wants and needs of others make a concentrated effort to return your focus back to being curious about your personal wants and needs which is how you will most reliably activate your intuition as concentrating on your specific needs helps clear the way to a direct connection.

Becoming aware of your intuition and acting on it are two very different things, however, which means that while you are first learning to trust your gut it is important that you also learn to observe when your intuition starts to pop up in a given situation. For example, if you are looking for a new job and come across one that fits your criteria in every way imaginable on paper, but doesn't feel quite right in practice, what would you do? If you are like most people you would turn down the job no matter what the benefits looked like, simply because something inside of you says it doesn't feel right.

In order to strengthen this feeling, you may want to write everything down in an intuition journal that will make it easier for you to notice future instances of your intuition doing its thing because you will be able to compare them to previous instances where something similar occurred. You will want to keep this journal close by and write down all your relevant experiences for at least a month until you are able to discern clear patterns. This will help you to get to know yourself more thoroughly and understand just how often intuition plays a role in your life.

Acting: Once you have gotten used to listening for your intuition, the next thing you are going to need to do is use it to make positive

Mental Toughness Mindset

changes to your actions which can be easier said than done. As it is not always clear what you need to do for your intuition to give you the all-clear. As such, when you are first getting started it doesn't matter what steps you take, if you get in the habit of taking them on the regular. These small steps can help you learn that listening to your intuition is beneficial until you eventually reach a point where listening to your intuition and reacting to it are essentially one in the same.

Stephen Patterson

Chapter 10:
Improve Your Mental Fortitude

Since its inception, mindfulness meditation been proven via scientific study to improve the physical wellbeing of those that practice it on a regular basis. At its heart, mindfulness meditation is all about focusing your mind to ensure that you are as fully aware of each moment as fully as possible. This, in turn, allows you to exist more completely in any given moment by expanding your consciousness to the fullest.

While it might sound like a tall order at first, the truth of the matter is that being mindful is a skill which means it can be improved by regular practice in much the same way as any other skill. Luckily, practicing mindfulness meditation is as easy as finding a few moments to focus solely on the present and the information that your senses are providing you now. In fact, if you can find just fifteen minutes a day to practice, you will soon find that your overall stress is likely to decrease, and your sense of self is likely to be at an all-time high. This isn't just an ephemeral feeling either, neuroimaging performed on those who practice mindfulness meditation on a regular basis shows that their minds actually process information more effectively, they are able to more easily regulate their emotions and their attention spans than those who do not make the practice a part of their daily routine.

Furthermore, the sooner you begin practicing mindfulness meditation, the greater the chance that doing so will ensure your brain retains more volume as you age, dramatically improving overall brain health as a result. This increased vitality also reaches the hippocampus which, in turn, makes it easier to learn and retain new information with minimal effort. At the same time, the amygdala becomes less active which means that the amount of fear, stress, and anxiety that you experience will be decreased as well.

Beyond the physical changes, regularly practicing mindfulness has been shown to decrease instances of participant's minds getting stuck in negative thought patterns while at the same time increasing focus. This should not come as a surprise given the fact that a recent Johns Hopkins study found that regularly practicing mindfulness meditation is equally effective at treating depression, ADD and anxiety. It also improves verbal reasoning skills as shown in a study which found that GRE students who practiced mindfulness performed up to 16 points better than their peers.

Bonus Benefits
- Practicing mindfulness has been shown to lower stress by decreasing the amount of the hormone cortisol the body produces.

- Practicing mindfulness can provide you with the opportunity to know the inner you and reveal ways to make yourself even better.

- Practicing mindfulness will help improve your ability to retain facts in both the short and long term.

- Practicing mindfulness will help keep you healthy. Those who regularly practice mindfulness meditation tend to report fewer sick days and that they recover from illnesses faster.

- Practicing mindfulness has been shown to improve the practitioner's ability to control their emotions and enhance their tolerance for pain.

- Practicing mindfulness can make music sound better. Those who meditate regularly often report an ability to more fully engage with music they hear and seem to enjoy it more.

- Practicing mindfulness will make you more empathetic towards others. Mindfulness meditation has been shown to make practitioners less judgmental, more compassionate and more active listeners.

Getting Started

While one of the best things about mindfulness meditation is its malleable nature, when you are first getting started it is recommended that you set some time aside each day to specifically devote to the practice. Ideally, this should be someplace that is quiet and during a period when you feel relaxed and where you can devote as much as thirty minutes to going deep within yourself without fear of worldly distractions. Remember, being mindful is all about creating space between the sensory information that your body is always sending to your mind and your reactions to that information so the fewer stimuli you have to deal with at the start, the easier you will find the practice to be.

Choose a set time and stick to it: As with any burgeoning habit, it is important that you create a routine for your mindfulness meditation and stay with it if you hope for the practice to stick. It typically takes 30 days for a new habit to take root in your daily schedule which is why it is important to commit fully to practicing mindfulness meditation if you ever want it to become part of your routine. Due to its low impact nature, nothing external is required, it is very easy for many people to make excuses to get out of meditating, especially if their daily schedule is already filled to bursting.

If you find yourself always coming up with an excuse to get out of meditating now, you may find the following piece of advice particularly useful. "Practice mindfulness meditation for fifteen minutes every day unless, of course, you are extremely busy in which case you should practice for thirty minutes instead." Don't let the outside world intrude on your potential for inner peace, find a time each day that works for you and stick with it no matter what; in a month's time, you will be glad you did.

Focus on the moment: While your end goal, while being mindful, should be to find a state of internal calm, regardless of what is going on in the world around you, it is difficult for most people to reach this state right away. Rather, they find it easier to start quieting their thoughts by focusing all their attention on the signals that their bodies are relaying to them now.

While, at first, you may not feel as though you are processing too much data from the world around you, especially if you are practicing in a quiet, calm space as suggested, this could not be further from the truth. The fact of the matter is that most of the time your brain filters out around 80 percent of the information it receives on a given day which means that information is there, you just need to get in the habit of accessing it regularly.

Over time, you will learn to tune out the thoughts you have regarding your everyday routines and instead tap directly into whatever it is that is going on around you. When you do so, it is important to process the information that your senses are providing you, while at the same time making a conscious effort to not pass judgement or dig too deeply into anything that crosses your mind. Judging results in additional thoughts, one way or another, which tend to lead to even more thoughts, until it is practically impossible for you to focus on the task at hand.

Remember, when it comes to mindfulness meditation, the goal is to get as close as you can manage to the moment as possible, which means ignoring everything else that is going on, except for what your senses are providing you. To reach this state, you will start by focusing on your breathing, especially on the way the air feels as it enters and exits your lungs, along with the way it smells and tastes.

Extend your senses outward, beyond your body to the room around you. Listen deeply and pick up the small sounds of the world around you that you are typically too busy to really hear. Notice the silence as well, just as important as the noise for its counterpoint. As with the thoughts you are keeping at bay, it is important to not do anything more with the sounds than simply accept them as they are. Don't pass judgement, don't use them to make assumptions about what is making them; simply let them wash over you and hear them in their purity.

From sounds, you should then move on to smells, strive to smell beyond the dominate smells in the room and pick up the fainter, more ingrained smells that you typically miss. Once more, the depth of the interaction should stop at registering the smell, proceed any farther down the path of interaction and you are no longer really in the moment. Acceptance of the stimuli you are receiving and cooperation with the universe at large should be your goal now, but this is no time to think about that.

Finally, bring the exercise back to a more internal point by considering any tastes that might be currently in your mouth. This is another instance that will require you to mentally turn off the filters that automatically diminish all sensation to the point of being manageable, don't let yourself accept that your mouth is currently barren, go deeper and find the taste that is truly there.

Once you cannot hold your focus any longer, gradually lose your control of the moment and let the world at large back in slowly, so as not to add too much stress back in too soon. Remember how you felt during the mediation, however, and strive to recreate that feeling in the world at large.

Extra Tips

Be consistent: This is probably the most difficult part of meditation. Without time, we find it easy to make an excuse to skip meditating for the day. Don't. Meditation doesn't require leaving your home or any kind of special equipment. All you need is your time and some space.

Observe the moment: Mindfulness is not necessarily quieting the mind or finding an eternal state of calmness. The goal here is simple. You want to pay attention to the moment you are in without judging. When you judge a thought or something you have done in the past, you tend to dwell on it. That isn't living in the moment and is not conducive to mindful meditation. While this is easier said than done, it is a crucial step to mindful meditation. With practice, it will be easy to achieve. Be mindful of the moment, of your senses and your surroundings.

Always come back to observation and the present moment: It is easy for our minds to get lost in thought. Mindfulness meditation is the art of bringing yourself back to the moment, over and over, as many times as it takes. Don't get discouraged. In the beginning, you will find your mind wanders a lot. Reel it back in and keep moving forward.

Be kind: Even if your mind does happen to wander, and it will don't be hard on yourself. It happens. Acknowledge whatever thoughts pop up, put them to the side and get back on track.

As you can see, the basics are quite simple. These are the things you need to remember daily while you are practicing. What's important is that you find the time to implement the basics every day. Mastering the basics will make it much simpler for you to dive into the deeper aspects of mindful meditation, which we will be discussing a little later.

Practice mindfulness during your Commute: Ensuring that you remain mindful during your commute will help you focus on the day ahead in such a way that you are sure to reach your destination calm, focused and ready to make the most of the time ahead. As being mindful is akin to being extremely present in each moment it will also ensure you are driving as safely as possible. By training your brain to stay in the present instead of thinking about the past or worrying about the future you, in turn, allow it to focus a substantial portion of energy on making the most of the now and getting the most from each work day.

Start as soon as you get into your vehicle by vocalizing your intention to be mindful during your morning commute. Then take a few deep breaths and use this time to become more aware of your body. Become aware of your hands on the steering wheel and what they feel beneath them. Become aware of your body and the sensations it feels as it is pressed against your seat. Feel your foot on the pedal and the resistance it feels as you prepare to drive. As you begin your drive take in the world around you while at the same time striving to be aware of the act of seeing, of the act of hearing. Try to focus on these three things, body, sights, sounds and only these things for the length of your drive.

That's really all there is to it, though like many things it is much easier said than done. Today's society is obsessed with multi-

Stephen Patterson

tasking and as such your mind will want to wander, thoughts will try and sneak their way in, you will want to think about the things waiting for you at work or tasks you left unfinished at home. Your phone will make at least one noise and you will be tempted to see the specifics of the notification. It is important to ignore these obstacles.

Chapter 11:
Improve Your Assertiveness

When it comes to learning to be assertive, everyone is going to come to the task with a different mindset and different expectations as to what the result will be. As such, the first step to becoming a more assertive individual is understanding just what assertiveness is and what it is not.

Unfortunately, what is and what is not assertive behavior is often muddled by the fact that, if you aren't careful, you can easily overstep the line and end up being aggressive rather than assertive. A person who is assertive when it comes to their needs is admired, a person who is aggressive for these same things is seen as a menace. Despite the serious differences between the two, it is still easy to confuse them, especially for those who are still learning about the finer points of assertiveness. As such, a definition of the two is useful in telling one from the other.

Assertiveness: At its heart, assertiveness is all about balance. It requires that you be in tune with yourself in order to accurately determine your wants and needs beforehand so that you can compare them to the wants and needs of those you meet. Those who are assertive are self-assured and confident and use that inner strength to get their point across in a way that be both fair and empathetic to the other person's point of view.

Aggressiveness: Aggressive behavior, on the other hand, is completely based around winning. Those who are aggressive rather than assertive are going to do what is in their own best interest without any thought for the desires, feelings, needs, and rights of others. Those who are aggressive use the personal power they might have for selfish gains and are often seen as bullying or pushy by others. They take what they want, when they want it and damn the consequences.

Focus on I statements: Statements that include sentiments such as "I want" or "I feel" make it easier for you to get your point across in a way that is both effective and clear. Additionally, the use of the word "I" should serve to let the other party know that perception is relative and what you are saying doesn't diminish whatever they are thinking or feeling. Furthermore, you will find that it helps you to keep the facts separate from whatever it is you want out of the scenario instead to help ensure you get the best possible outcome each time.

Escalate properly: If you find that your first attempt at being assertive fails, then you may need to consider escalating your approach significantly if you wish to get your point across. This will include things like taking a firm, yet respectful, tone while still working to be polite. This is not the same as increasing the emotional intensity of the conversation as this will just make you seem aggressive, put the other person on the defensive, and ultimately do little to solve whatever the real problem of the moment might be. This is a fine line to walk and learning to do so successfully is something that will only happen with practice which is why it is important to try to do as much practice as possible.

Consider scripting: Scripting is a useful means of getting started practicing being assertive if you aren't comfortable with the practice as it will allow you to figure out just what you were going to say in advance so there is little question as to what you will do next. In order to find the perfect thing to say you will want to start by focusing on the specific event that is taking place. This means you will want to break things down exactly how you see the problem as well as what you see the most likely solution to be.

From there, the next thing you are going to want to think about it is the way the situation currently makes you feel. This will make it easier for you to come to a decision when it comes to the best way to express your feelings while at the same time ensuring that your response isn't seen as a criticism or judgement of the other person. Keep in mind that making your feelings clear is the only way you can express to the other person how important that whatever you are requesting come to pass which is what you will be discussing when it comes to talking about your needs. This will also make it possible for you to guarantee that the person you are speaking with knows exactly where you are going from so that you can be confident that there are no misunderstandings between you.

This also leaves them free to choose a response that most clearly adheres to their response to your intended meaning. It is also important to clearly indicate what it is you want the results of your request to be, either the benefits that go along with your plan or the consequences of going against it. Choosing the right tactic is an important part of ensuring that your assertive plea is also persuasive.

Anger is acceptable: One of the most difficult things for many people to do when they are learning to become assertive is understand that expressing that you are angry is different than expressing yourself in an angry fashion. The truth of the matter is that anger doesn't have to be an inherently negative thing and it is sometimes a very natural response to a given situation. People who have a problem with anger have a problem expressing it in an effective may. If you can manage to express your anger is a way that is free of excessive negativity then it can be as healthy as any other emotion. Remember, understanding that all your feelings are valid is an important part of becoming assertive.

Ensure your requests are clear: When it comes to doing everything in your power to ensure that each of your assertive requests is met with an appropriate response, it is important to do what you can to ensure that those requests are done in a way that is both rational and clear. A request that is assertive in a positive way is one that is straight to the point while also taking clear steps to no make the other party feel inferior in any way. This is essentially the opposite of a passive-aggressive request which is often directly designed to hurt the recipient while also allowing the person who said it to hide behind a veil of innocence.

Validate your requests: In order to ensure you remain assertive rather than aggressive it is important to take an extra moment to always try and understand just where the other party is coming from. If you can understand the feelings that the other party is trying to express, then it becomes much easier for them to understand where you are coming from as well. This is not the same as agreeing with them, however, and should instead just do wonders when it comes to making them feel as though you are really listening which should, in theory, make it easier for you to get your way without being seen as aggressive.

When listening to what the other person has to say it is crucial that you do what you can to come across as respectful in both your verbal and nonverbal words and actions. This attitude of openness and respect can help the other person feel more relaxed and thus more likely to give in to your way of thinking. To help with this it is important to always retain eye contact and to truly listen to what the other party has to say if you truly hope to find the type of solution that is best for everyone.

Posture matters: It doesn't matter what it is you are trying to be assertive about, you are going to come off as more persuasive if you say it with your shoulders squared and your back straight. When you speak you are going to want to always look straight ahead which signals that you are always willing to face the reaction to the things you are saying. This will also show the person you are speaking with that you are willing to face their conversation head on while also looking for a reaction that is largely positive.

While working on the above it is also important that you work to look as relaxed as possible because there is nothing that will kill the positive vibes you have created like looking tense. Looking this way either means you are lying or are looking for a fight, neither or which is something that is likely to put another person in a good mood. Looking relaxed, on the other hand, also makes it easier for you to look confident, which will make it more likely the other party will go along with what you have to say as a result.

When you are speaking with another person directly you will also want to take steps to ensure your body is physically aligned with theirs as well. At the bare minimum, you should stand or sit, depending on what they are doing, though if you are standing then you will want to take the extra step of planting your feet at shoulder width to show the other party that you aren't hiding anything. What's more, this will also help you looked more relaxed and retain specific details more easily.

While you are talking to the other party you will find success if you try and slowly copy the gestures and mannerisms they use. This will serve to not only help them feel more at ease but will also help make it more likely that any assertive suggestions you make are received in a positive fashion. You will be able to tell that you have fully convinced them to think about things your way when you can stop mimicking their body movements and they start mimicking what you are doing instead.

Hands and arms: When it come to your arms and your hands, the most important thing to keep in mind is that you should only take an action if it looks natural. If you make the mistake of overthinking things then you will end up stifling their fluidity, leaving you with something that feels forced, awkward and of no good to anyone. Essentially what this means is that if you don't naturally gesture all that much regularly it is not something you need to force as a bad gesture is much worse than no gesture at all.

As it is with your posture, your goal with your arms and hands should be to look as relaxed as you can always. If you are being assertive about a reasonable request then you should have no reason to be nervous, after all. Above everything else, however, it is important that you never stand with your arms crossed unless you want to give off that very specific type of message. Standing in that way shows that you are disinterested in working towards a group consensus and only want things to be your way or the highway.

In order to be assertive in an appropriate way, you will want to stand so that your arms naturally hang by your side. This will indicate to those you are speaking with that you are looking to come to a real consensus which means listening to what others have to say as opposed to just getting your own way. You will want to avoid having balled fists while doing so, however, and if you are sitting you will want to avoid placing both of your palms facedown as well. Both these actions indicate that you don't like the current state of the conversation and that you are feeling angry.

Even if you do not express yourself using hand movements it is still important that you take the time to cultivate a quality handshake. A good handshake is a crucial part of making a good first impression which can then be capitalized on when it comes time to be assertive. The ideal handshake is one that is firm without being aggressive. Anything that is more over-the-top than that is only an indication that you are looking to dominate the other person which is not the message you really want to send in most instances. On the other hand, adopting a limp handshake will tell the other person that they are in control which can make it more difficult to get you way when being assertive in the long run.

Chapter 12:
Improve Your Ability to Set Goals Successfully

In order to ensure that you can plan effectively, you are going to want to start by choosing the right types of goals to make sure you find the type of success you are looking for. The best way to do this is to make sure that the goals you set are SMART goals and then set sub-goals based on the broad goals that you have decided upon.

Smart goals are specific: A goal which is specific is almost twice as likely to be accomplished than one which is general. A truly specific goals can answer a series of definite questions.

- Who will be involved in achieving the goal?

- What, specifically, is the goal being set to accomplish?

- Where will the completion of the goal take place?

- When will the goal realistically be completed by?

- Which requirements or constraints around the goal will make it challenging to complete?

- Why does the goal need accomplishing and what will the benefit of doing so be?

SMART goals are measurable: A goal which is measurable makes it easy to determine precise metrics for success, progress or failure. Keeping goals measurable will help you and your teamwork through them at a steady pace rather than in fits and starts. If you are having a hard time making your goals measurable, try considering how many or how much of something might indicate success or failure. Likewise, starting from the endpoint and working backwards may be easier, consider how you will know the goal has been successfully completed and then working towards the beginning can make measure goals easier

The best way to keep your goals measurable is to set up a generalized timetable based on whatever it is that you have planned for yourself and then keep track of how you are doing in relation to it. This timetable won't need to be extremely precise, if it has specific deadlines that you can always actively be working towards than it is doing its job. Keeping tabs on your success in chunks will ensure that you not only start off on the right foot but keep that success up all the way through to the finish line as well.

SMART goals are attainable: A good goal is one that is realistically attainable which means that you understand any potential roadblocks that may stand between you and the goal in question and that they will be ultimately surmountable. This means you are going to want to take a good hard look at your goal from all sides and be realistic with yourself about your chances for success. While looking at your goal through rose colored glasses might make you feel better, it is truly in your best interest to be as critical during this step as possible.

The trick here is to pick a goal that is attainable enough to keep you working diligently at it, while not so easy that it wouldn't make sense to have sub-goals surrounding completing it successfully. While 20 years out might be a bit excessive for your current needs, everyone can benefit from a good five-year plan. If you land on a goal that is either too difficult to achieve or too easy to warrant striving towards you will find it much for difficult to work to achieve it successfully.

SMART goals are realistic: A good goal is one that is realistic in addition to being attainable which means that you can expect success without something extremely unlikely being required to push reality into your favor. An ideal goal is one that is going to require a good amount of work to achieve, while remaining not so difficult as to become unrealistic. Additionally, you are going to want to shy away from goals that you can meet without putting for any real amount of effort as goals that are too easy can actually be demotivating as it then becomes easy to continue putting them off and putting them off until they eventually fade into oblivion.

SMART goals are timely: A good goal is one that as a clear timetable for when it is going to be completed. Even the best-intentioned goals are likely to fall apart if their timetable is to strict, but also if it is too generous. Timetables that are too condensed increase the odds of requiring you too cut corners in order to find success while those that are too long can be beset by unexpected complications that would have been avoided had the timetable been a little shorter.

Finding the right timeframe is key to keeping your motivation levels at the right point to ensure success in a reasonable period.

What this means is that you will want to determine what your goal will be, determine a timeline for completion, and then do the same for each of the sub-goals you set as well. When it comes to setting a due date for your goals, you will want to consider periods of time that are long enough to allow you to realistically experience a few setbacks along the way, without being so lax that you never actually get around to accomplishing anything. What you are shooting for is something that will force you to stop dreaming about financial freedom and start working towards it, not something so strict that you have no realistic chance of success.

Determining assumptions and constraints: After you have an objective in place, the next thing you will need to include will be the constraints and assumptions as the three together will provide you with the general scope you are looking to do.

When it comes to determining assumptions, you will want to make a list of all the things that you are going to assume to be true when it comes to the planning stage. This includes things like being able to acquire the resources you need to complete the goal and find people who can help you as required. You will also want to make assumptions when it comes to the length of time each stage of the project will take, that other projects will finish on time, etc.

When listing out your assumptions, it is important to be realistic as well. This means you can assume you will have the time to complete your goal, but not that you will have so much time to devote to it that you can expect it to get done more quickly than average. Listing out your assumptions can be a slippery slope, simply because it can be easy to lose the line between what you know will happen and what you want to happen, so it is important to remain vigilant. If any of your assumptions aren't 100 percent guaranteed to come to pass, then you will want to ensure you have a backup plan in place as well to ensure you don't end up wasting any time.

When making your list of constraints, you are only going to want to list out those things that you know, for a fact, that you are going to have to work around. While you may find that constraints make the goal more complicated to achieve having a clear idea of what you are up against right from the start will only help to make things simpler in the long-term.

Implementation: After your SMART Goals have been decided upon, it is a good idea to try and generalize all the goals into five primary ones which can be easily focused on. The fewer the number of goals the more likely they will be acted upon in a reasonable frame of time. If goals cannot be easily generalized, it is important to instead start with the ones that will make the most difference and then work down the list from there. Regardless of what you settle on, it is important to ensure each goal has a means for easily keeping track of its progress.

Decide on tactics: For each goal, you will want to consider how it can best be completed by slotting it into your current schedule. This process should include enough consideration to ensure that tactics and goals align. Tactics are likely to change as the goal heads towards success and should be studied to ensure they remain appropriate for the goal in question.

Act: After tactics have been decided upon, it is time to put them into practice. This is the stage where the rubber hits the road, quality goals should always require total buy-in to be their most successful.

Review as needed: Once the action is in progress it is important to monitor and change the action as needed. The best goals are constantly being improved and your goals and the implementation thereof should be no exception.

Understand the difference between ambition and goals: When you first begin working to improve the quality of the goals you set it is important to frame your goals in a realistic manner. As previously stated, the human mind works best when it can link effort with the reward which means setting yourself up with an unreasonable ambition is a recipe for disaster. As such it is important that you have both general ambitions about the skill plus specific goals that you can meet on a regular basis. For example, learning to speak French fluently is an ambition, which if it is your only goal will cause you to give up long before you obtain it. However, if you instead make it your goal to learn 100 new French words every week, that is a goal which can be objectively accomplished in a reasonable period.

Try the 80/20 principle: Also known as the Pareto principle, the 80/20 principle is a simple ratio that explains the idea that 80 percent of your results come from 20 percent of your effort. This is a common refrain among sales teams but is equally true of many languages, including English. 20 percent of the words are repeated 80 percent of the time; it is the same with pop music. This principle can be applied to learning if you first take the time to understand with reasonable surety what the most important 20 percent of a topic is. Again, it is important to only apply this principal when you can be more than 75 percent sure you understand what the most important 20 percent of a topic to be. Remember, a little knowledge is a dangerous thing.

Stephen Patterson

Conclusion

Just because you've finished this book doesn't mean there is nothing left to learn on the topic, and expanding your horizons is the only way to find the mastery you seek.

With so many different aspects of your mindset to work on, it can be tempted to start on all of them at once. This is only likely to lead to failure, however, which is why it is a far better choice to start with the aspect of the mental toughness mindset that is most important to you, or the one that seems as though it will have the greatest immediate benefit in your life instead. Doing so will give you the single-minded focus to not only learn to access that aspect of the mindset but to master it as well.

What's more, it is important to keep in mind that while the means of doing so are relatively straightforward, changing even the simplest aspect of your mindset is going to take plenty of hard work and determination if you want it to stick. As such, it can be thought of like a marathon rather than a sprint which means that slow and steady will win the race every time.

If you find this book helpful in anyway a review to support my endeavors is much appreciated.

Mental Toughness Mindset

Stephen Patterson

Printed in the USA
CPSIA information can be obtained
at www.ICGtesting.com
CBHW021609190424
7209CB00042B/1004